THE RUIN OF GILBERT'S PRIZED BLUE HUMMER

Annie Starks-Johnson

AuthorHouse™
1663 Liberty Drive
Bloomington, IN 47403
www.authorhouse.com
Phone: 1-800-839-8640

First published by AuthorHouse 6/16/2009

ISBN: 978-1-4389-8029-4 (sc)

Library of Congress Control Number: 2009905903

Printed in the United States of America
Bloomington, Indiana

This book is printed on acid-free paper.

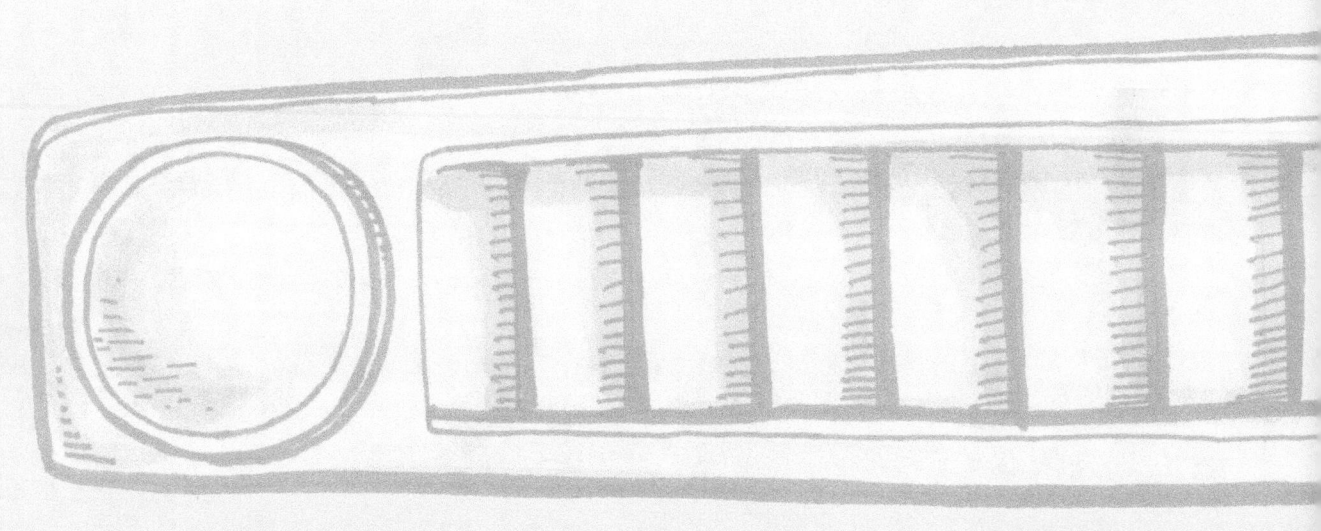

Bugsy wanted to surprise Gilbert, his owner, and take his most prized blue Hummer to the car wash. "Come on Nafisa, let's do it," Bugsy said.

"Do you know how much trouble we will be in if anything happens to his Hummer?" Nafisa squealed.

"Oh, don't whimp out on me now, Nafisa, it's just a car wash. What could happen just driving it through the car wash?" Bugsy shouted.

Devo was listening to the conversation between Bugsy and Nafisa.

"Hey you guys," Devo interrupted, I don't think Dottie would like that idea."

"Who's going to tell her?" Bugsy exclaimed.

"Not I," Nafisa answered quickly.

"Well, I don't see a problem then," Bugsy boasted.

"I've never been to a car wash before," Devo said, sounding worried, "but I'm not staying behind."

"It's fun," Bugsy said, not admitting that he hadn't been to a car wash either. Nor had he driven a car before. "All right, let's do this," he shouted with enthusiasm.

They all ran toward the blue Hummer and jumped in.

"Nafisa, you drive, and Devo, you get in the front seat with Nafisa. I need more leg space, so I will get in the back seat," Bugsy said in an authoritative voice.

They all fastened their seat belts. Nafisa started up the Hummer and headed to the car wash.

"Turn on the radio Nafisa," Bugsy said as he jumped up and down in the middle of the back seat.

"OK, Bugsy, get a grip," Nafisa replied in an agitated voice.

"Let the top down too! It's a convertible!" Bugsy was bouncing up and down and swaying from side to side.

"I must admit, this is a cool Hummer," Nafisa squealed in her high-pitched voice.

"Slow down, Nafisa!" Bugsy yelled. "The car wash is right on the next corner. Just pull in there, and I will show you what to do."

Nafisa followed Bugsy's instructions and drove the blue Hummer into the car wash.

"OK, just select the wash you want and it will do the rest," Bugsy ordered.

"Let's give it the works!" Nafisa shouted. "We'll get it washed, waxed, and polish the wheels! Oh yeah! Gilbert will be so proud of us when he sees the shiny chrome wheels!"

"Bugsy, this was a great idea after all," Devo added.

Nafisa, pushed the button, and the big conveyor belt slowly pulled the car inside toward the big brushes that eagerly awaited the blue Hummer

"What are those things?" Bugsy shouted.

"What do you mean?" Nafisa asked. "Haven't you done this before?"

"Not exactly," Bugsy replied as he slumped to the floor in the back-seat of the car.

"It's too late now!" Nafisa shouted.

Bugsy let out a loud yelp and leaped to the floor of the blue Hummer. He buried his head under the driver's seat as far as he could go.

Water came gushing in from all directions, and the big brushes were spinning around the car making mounds of suds with every stroke.

"Somebody forgot to let the top up!" Nafisa yelled as she struggled with the twirling brushes and sudsy water.

They were all making gurgling sounds, as they fought off the forceful water with both hands.

Finally the water stopped, and they didn't feel the strong force of the big twirling brushes anymore. Nafisa and Devo opened their eyes slowly, as they turned around to see if Bugsy was all right.

When they didn't see him they both panicked. "Where is Bugsy, Nafisa?" Devo asked with a panicked voice.

"Oh Devo!" Nafisa cried. "Where could he be?"

Suddenly Bugsy raised his head, shaking himself free from the water. He was coughing and sneezing while trying to regain his composure after the traumatic car wash experience.

"Bugsy, are you all right?" Nafisa asked.

"What happened?" Bugsy asked, still in a disoriented state.

"Oh Bugsy, we have destroyed Gilbert's beautiful blue Hummer." Devo said.

"He will never forgive me!" Bugsy cried. "Never in a million years!"

They all climbed out of the car with sad faces not knowing how they were going to explain to Gilbert that they had ruined his blue Hummer.

"Bugsy, it's not all your fault. We should have talked you out of it," Nafisa said. "Together we will find a way to break the news to Gilbert."

Suddenly they heard pounding foot steps rapidly approaching them.

They all turned to see what was coming, and saw Gilbert and Dottie running frantically toward them.

The look on Gilbert's face was one of a ferocious bull charging a matador who was waving a red flag.

"We're in so much trouble!" Bugsy shouted.

"What shall we do now, Bugsy?" Nafisa squealed.

"We have to accept the consequences for our actions, Bugsy said in a very scared voice. It's not going to be an easy one."

Gilbert and Dottie finally caught up to them. Gilbert took one look at his prized blue Hummer, and he let out a loud yelp. "Who's responsible for this!"

"We all are," Nafisa answered.

"It's ruined! I can never restore it! Never!" Gilbert shouted as he buried his face in his hands.

"Gilbert," Dottie interrupted. "Let's assess the damage to see how bad things really are."

"What's the use?" Gilbert moaned. "Just look at it!"

"Everything will be all right. You will see, Gilbert," Dottie said in a soft, consoling voice.

Dottie got busy searching for antique car restoration specialists. She wanted to find the best people to restore Gilbert's prized blue Hummer.

About two days after Dottie's search began, she received a reply from a Hummer specialist. He invited her to come to his shop to see some of his restoration projects.

When Dottie arrived, to her surprise, there was a blue Hummer almost identical to Gilbert's blue Hummer. "This is perfect!" She exclaimed.

"Hello Dottie, my name is Johnny," said the Hummer specialist. "I would be honored to do business with you. Give me a month, and I'm sure Gilbert will be a happy customer."

"You have the job," Dottie said.

Dottie ran off to find Gilbert. She wanted to give him the good news.

She found Gilbert in the garage sitting beside his blue Hummer. He was starring at it in disbelief. Gilbert had a sad look on his face like a little boy who had lost his very best friend.

"Gilbert," Dottie called out in a soft voice. "I found a specialist to restore your blue Hummer."

"Oh Dottie it will never be the same again." Gilbert wailed, never lifting his face to look at Dottie.

"It is going to be better than before. I promise," Dottie said.

Johnny had the blue Hummer towed to his shop and began the restoration. Johnny loved his work, but he wanted to do something really special for Gilbert.

Johnny worked diligently restoring the blue Hummer, and the time passed quickly. Two weeks had gone by, and he was already down to the finishing touches. He walked around the blue Hummer admiring the work that he had done. He was very pleased. To his amazement this was his best work by far. "I think Gilbert will be very happy," he thought with a big smile of approval on his face.

Johnny called Dottie to arrange a delivery date for Gilbert's blue Hummer.

When the time came, Johnny drove the Hummer to show his handiwork. Dottie and Gilbert, along with Bugsy, Devo, and Nafisa, were anxiously awaiting his arrival.

When Gilbert saw his prized possession, he was so excited. He could not believe his eyes. "It's like new! Dottie you were so right! It's better than before."

Gilbert turned to Bugsy, Devo, and Nafisa. "I forgive you guys.

I know you didn't ruin my blue Hummer on purpose, but I hope that you all have learned a valuable lesson. You should always respect the property of others."

"We have learned our lesson, and we have also learned that we should not follow others if we don't agree with what they are doing," Nafisa said.